DATE DUE			
FE 16 '89	FE 13 '9	OC 19 '92	APR 25 '9
AP 7 '89	FE 28 '9	MY 6 '93	JL 25 '9
MY 9 '89	AP 6 '9	JY 1 '93	SEP 05 '9
JY 7 '89	MY 11 '9	JY 7 '93	JE 07 '00
JY 27 '8	JY 5 '91	FEB 11 '94	AG 29 '00
SE 1 8	AG 01 '91	JUN 8 '00	MR 19 '0
OC 3 '89	AG 15 '9	JUL 30 '94	JE 26 '0
NO 11 '89	OC 1 '9	OCT 28 '94	AG 1 '74
NO 29 '8	OC 31 '91	NOV 25 '94	FE 12 '0
DE 22 '89	DE 16 '9	JAN 18 '9	JY 15 '0
JE 29 '90	JE 29 '92	JUN 2 3	JY 29 '88
JY 25 '90	JY 15 '92	SEP 02 '9	

AG 0 4 '74

E
Dis

Disney Productions
Goofy's book of colors

Walt Disney Productions
presents

Goofy's Book

of Colors

Random House 🏠 New York

[Lib]rary of Congress Cataloging in Publication Data: Main entry under title: Walt
[Di]sney Productions presents Goofy's book of colors.
[(W]isney's wonderful world of reading ; #52) SUMMARY: Goofy introduces the basic
[co]lors as he paints several objects, and shows how primary colors combine to form other
[co]lors such as green and purple.
[1.] Color] I. Walt Disney Productions. II. Title: Goofy's book of colors. III. Series.
[?]7.G637 1983 [E] 82-18630 ISBN: 0-394-85734-8 (trade); 0-394-95734-2 (lib.
[bd]g.) Manufactured in the United States of America 1 2 3 4 5 6 7 8 9 0

red

Goofy the painter has
a **red** truck with **red** wheels.
In the truck is a can
of **red** paint.
What else in the picture
is **red**?

red light

safety flag

truck

Mickey Mouse calls hello to Goofy.
What color is Mickey's tongue?

yellow

Goofy is painting the fence **yellow**.
He stops to sniff the **yellow** sunflowers.

sunflowers

fence

chicks

canary

Minnie brings Goofy
a bowl of fruit.
Do you know which
fruits are **yellow**?
What else do you see
that is **yellow**?

butterfly

hair bow

lemon

pear

banana

dress

daffodils

shoes

blue

Goofy has just painted
Pluto's doghouse **blue**.
"A beautiful job,"
says Donald Duck.
"Woof!" says Pluto.
He likes it too.

butterfly

blue jay

doghouse

dish

PLUTO

hat

flowers

sailor suit

blue jeans

Donald is wearing
his **blue** sailor suit.
What else is **blue**?

green

Oops! Goofy knocked over a can of
blue paint and a can of yellow paint.
The colors mixed together and made **green**.
Blue and yellow make **green**.
What **green** things do you see?

vest

tree

cap

door

bike

shirt

wagon

grass

frog

orange

tractor

shirt

Goofy is painting Clarabelle's
tractor **orange**.
Red and yellow make **orange**.

"You must be thirsty," says Clarabelle. "Have some **orange**ade."

pumpkins

orangeade

curtains

dress

Which flowers are **orange**?

shoes

flowers

purple

hot-air balloon

Goofy and Mickey are
mixing some **purple** paint.
Blue and red make **purple**.

Here come Daisy and Dewey with
some **purple** things in their baskets.
Can you name them?
Which of Dewey's balloons
are **purple**?

balloons

hair bow

dress

grapes

shoes

eggplant

violets

brown

Look what Pluto did!
He kicked over three cans of paint!

cat

fence

tree bark

The three colors mixed together and
made a new color.
Yellow, red, and blue make **brown**.
What do you see that is **brown**?

bird

cows

Pluto

black

car

nose

ears

Goofy is painting his car **black**.

Then he is going to light a charcoal fire and have a barbecue.

Charcoal is **black**.

If food burns on the barbecue grill, it is **black** too!

crows

fence

cat

shovel

barbecue grill

charcoal

clouds

white

dog

duck

snow

Goofy wants to paint his house **white**—
as **white** as snow.
But it is too cold to paint today.
So Goofy has built a snowman.

tooth

gloves

snowman

What do you see that is **white**?

gray

The lamppost outside the zoo is **gray**.
Goofy is giving it a new coat of paint.
He mixes black and white to get **gray**.

rhinoceros

rock

lamppost

elephant

birds

stone wall

mouse

Do you know these
big **gray** zoo animals?

pink

dollhouse

curtains

roses

doll

lollipop

pig

Goofy paints the dollhouse **pink**.
He mixes red and white together
to make **pink**.
Do you see any other **pink** toys?

Goofy painted
a rainbow.

red   orange   yellow   green

Can you name the colors
in the rainbow?

blue   purple